Earlywine Media Center
Date Due

1	13
2	14
3	15
4	16
5	17
6	18
7	19
8	20
9	21
10	22
11	23
12	24

OCT 16 2007

EARLYWINE ELEMENTARY

So You Want to
Be an
EXPLORER?

So You Want to Be an EXPLORER?

Judith St. George

Illustrated by
David Small

PHILOMEL BOOKS

Patricia Lee Gauch, editor

PHILOMEL BOOKS
A division of Penguin Young Readers Group
Published by The Penguin Group
Penguin Group (USA) Inc., 375 Hudson Street, New York, NY 10014, U.S.A.   Penguin Group (Canada), 10 Alcorn Avenue, Toronto,
Ontario, Canada M4V 3B2 (a division of Pearson Penguin Canada Inc.)   Penguin Books Ltd, 80 Strand, London WC2R 0RL, England.
Penguin Ireland, 25 St. Stephen's Green, Dublin 2, Ireland (a division of Penguin Books Ltd.)   Penguin Group (Australia), 250 Camberwell
Road, Camberwell, Victoria 3124, Australia (a division of Pearson Australia Group Pty Ltd).   Penguin Books India Pvt Ltd, 11 Community
Centre, Panchsheel Park, New Delhi - 110 017, India.   Penguin Group (NZ), Cnr Airborne and Rosedale Roads, Albany, Auckland 1310,
New Zealand (a division of Pearson New Zealand Ltd).   Penguin Books (South Africa) (Pty) Ltd, 24 Sturdee Avenue, Rosebank,
Johannesburg 2196, South Africa.   Penguin Books Ltd, Registered Offices: 80 Strand, London WC2R 0RL, England.

Book design by Semadar Megged. The text is set in Golden Type ITC.   The art was done in ink, watercolor, and pastel chalk.

Library of Congress Cataloging-in-Publication Data
St. George, Judith, date.   So you want to be an explorer? / Judith St. George ; illustrated by David Small.   p. cm.
Includes bibliographical references.   1. Explorers—Juvenile literature. 2. Discoveries in geography—Juvenile literature. 3. Adventure and
adventurers—Juvenile literature. I. Small, David, 1945- ill. II. Title.   G175.S7 2005   910'.9–dc22   2004027239
ISBN 0-399-23868-9
10 9 8 7 6 5 4 3 2 1
First Impression

You say that you're plucky, like a thrill or two, and are always game for something new? How about sailing unknown seas to new lands . . . or climbing a mountain in a blizzard . . . or making your way through a pitch-black cave?

If you shout, "That's for me!" then the life of an explorer might be just the life for you. You've probably already figured out that explorers are adventuresome and gutsy. But do you know what else makes them tick?

Explorers have a middle name—Curiosity.

Seventeen-year-old Marco Polo was a curious kid. In 1271 he waved So Long to Italy and headed for Asia to see the sights. Some sights! Ladies in trousers, paper money, teeth of gold, emeralds and rubies. How long did Marco snoop around Asia? Only twenty-four years.

British Mary Kingsley was curious about Africa, especially cannibal life. In the 1890s, she traveled alone through unexplored Africa. She studied the cannibals, and they studied her. With her bonnets and umbrellas, Ms. Mary looked like a proper lady. But under her long skirts? Men's trousers.

Explorers tackle a quest with gusto.

"Great" wasn't added to Alexander's name for nothing. In 334 B.C. he began a quest to scout, explore—and conquer—the known world. Botanists, geographers, astronomers and engineers tagged along. In eleven years, King Alex the Great founded seventy cities and a world-wide empire.

Norwegian Thor Heyerdahl's quest was to prove that Westerners could have sailed from Peru to Polynesia thousands of years ago. Thor built a balsa wood raft in 1947, named it *Kon-Tiki* and made the same Pacific voyage. Proof positive for Thor . . . and everyone else.

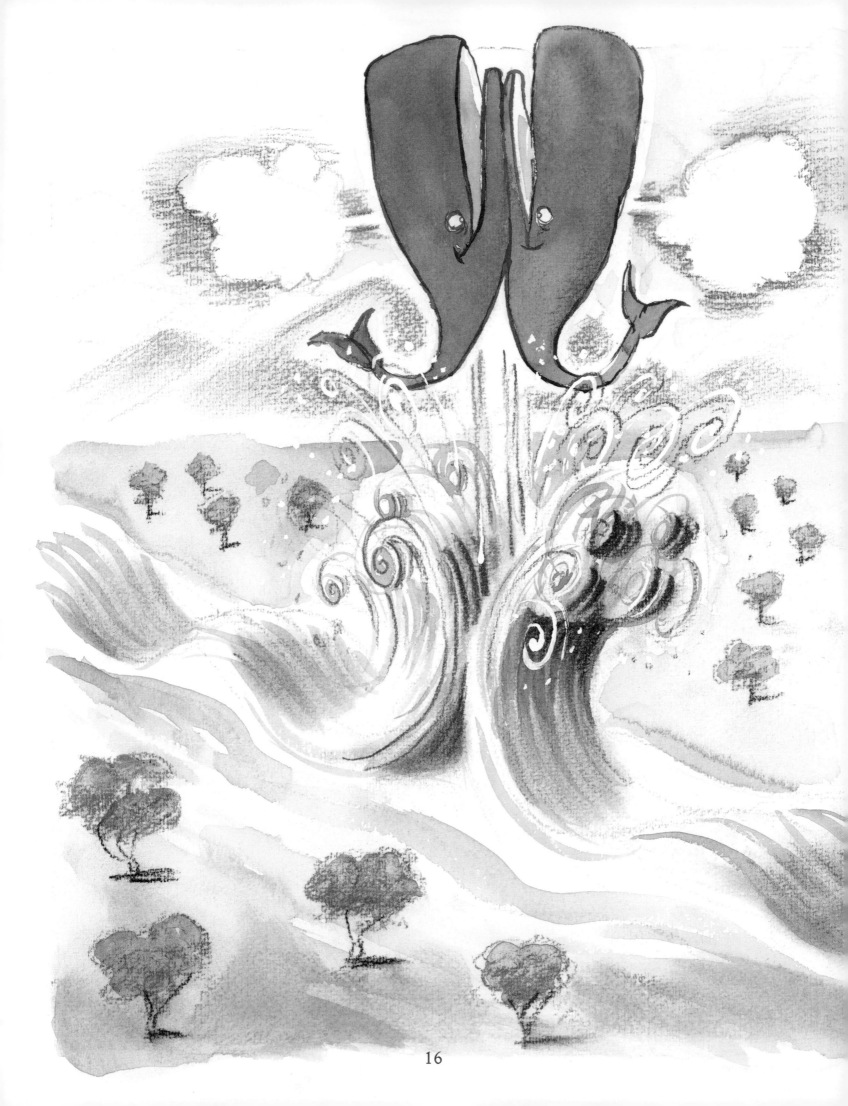

Explorers are a determined bunch.

Was Ferdinand Magellan stubborn? You bet he was. He spent a year trying to sail from the Atlantic to the Pacific. Finally, in 1520 he sailed from one ocean to the other through a strait at the tip of South America— the Strait of Magellan. (The water was salty in both.)

Robert Peary was gung ho to reach the North Pole first. On his fifth crack at it in 1909, Commander Peary, his steadfast companion African-American Matthew Henson, and four Inuits finally succeeded. But the cold was a nightmare. Commander P. lost eight toes to frostbite.

Like it or not, explorers are risk takers.

Barbara Washburn was hardly a risk taker. She was an office secretary. Then she risked climbing up two never-before-climbed Alaskan mountains. Good-bye, office. Barbara's all-time risk? In 1947 she was the first woman to stand on top of North America's highest peak—Mt. McKinley.

Talk about risk! Country boy Chuck Yeager soared into the Army Air Corps' wild blue yonder at eighteen and never came down. First a hotshot World War II ace and then a test pilot, Chuck zoomed the first jet through the sound barrier in 1947 and wowed the world.

19

Good explorers respect the natives.

Geographer Heinrich Barth's home-away-from-home in the 1850s? The Sahara Desert. Heinrich lived and made friends with the Arabs, mastered their language and wore what they wore. With his native know-how, he explored thousands of miles of desert . . . and lived to tell the tale.

In 1911 Norwegian Roald Amundsen raced Englishman Robert Scott to the South Pole. Roald learned from the native Inuits what food to eat—how to make animal-skin clothing—build igloos—manage sled dogs—prevent frostbite—cure snow blindness. Robert didn't. The winner? Roald.

Bad explorers can do the natives in.

In the 1400s, Portuguese seamen explored Africa's west coast. They did more than explore. They captured African natives to sell as slaves. Across the ocean, gold-hungry Spanish explorers slaughtered thousands of Aztec and Inca natives for their gold.

Explorers need maps, and mapmakers need explorers.

Italian-born Amerigo Vespucci sailed to South America in 1499. Boy, did he get around. He explored rivers, harbors and 3,330 miles of coastline. Mapmakers worked like crazy to draw new maps of the world. Amerigo's reward? The New World was named for him—America.

In the early 1900s British Gertrude Bell galloped across the Arabian Desert—sidesaddle. "Daughter of the Desert" Gertrude mapped unexplored sands. During World War I, she was a friend-in-need. She mapped vital desert water wells and railroad lines for the British.

Explorers can launch a whole new sport—got any ideas?

In 1760 scientist Horace de Saussure offered prize money to the first to climb Europe's highest mountain, Mont Blanc. (Dragons lived there.) Two men made it to the top. (There were no dragons.) Sports lovers have been clambering up mountains ever since.

Civil War Major John Wesley Powell was first to explore the Grand Canyon's rivers in 1869. He and his men hung on to their four boats for dear life through some thousand miles of whirlpools, jagged rocks, rapids and pounding waves. Now people go white-water rafting for sport.

Explorers can make mistakes like anyone else.

Bjarni Herjolfsson sailed for Greenland in 986. Lost in a fog, he sighted a wooded coastline. He knew it wasn't Greenland, so he didn't stop. Leif Eriksson later followed Bjarni's same route and did stop. Who got credit for landing first in North America? Leif Eriksson, that's who.

All Hernando de Soto cared about was finding gold for Spain. In 1541 he was the first European to cross the Mississippi River. What a muddy nuisance—not worth exploring. In 1682, René-Robert de La Salle traveled down the same Mississippi River . . . and snatched up all the land for France.

No matter what explorers discover, not everyone believes them.

In 320 B.C., Greek trader Pytheas sailed north almost to the Arctic Circle. The sun was out all night. Pytheas reported: "The sun shines at midnight." He saw icebergs. "The seas are curdled," he announced. People jeered. Are you crazy, Pytheas? (He wasn't.)

Cowboy Jim White explored a New Mexico cave in 1898. What fantastic rock formations, gigantic chambers and miles of passageways. But everyone pooh-poohed Cowboy Jim's stories. Then a photographer took pictures. Oops! Jim was right. People have lined up to tour Carlsbad Caverns ever since.

How about being first to go around the world in almost anything?

Ferdinand Magellan's crew and ship, *Victoria*, circled the globe, but Magellan lost his life on the way. (1519–1522)

Joshua Slocum made the voyage alone in his sloop, *Spray*. (1895–1898)

Thomas Stevens pedaled his way around on a Columbia high-wheel bicycle. (1884–1887)

For his circuit, Hugo Eckener captained an airship, *Graf Zeppelin*. (1930)

Wiley Post flew the circle in his airplane, the *Winnie Mae*. (1933)

American sailors circumnavigated underwater in a nuclear-powered submarine, *Triton*. (1960)

Yuri Gagarin orbited the earth in a spacecraft, *Vostok I*. (1961)

David Kunst completed the loop the hard way—on his own two feet. (1970–1974)

Ted Simon bombed around the world on his Triumph motorcycle. (1973–1977)

Bertrand Piccard and Brian Jones drifted the distance in a hot-air balloon, *Breitling Orbiter 3*. (1999)

Explorers need to keep a sharp eye on their companions.

In 1513 Spanish conquistador Vasco Núñez de Balboa marched across Panama, the first European to see the Pacific Ocean. His trusted lieutenant Francisco Pizarro went with him. Trusted? Hah! Pizarro later had Balboa arrested and executed on a false charge of treason.

English navigator Henry Hudson put to sea in search of the Northwest Passage to China. Instead, he discovered an American river, bay and strait. (Later all named Hudson.) But in 1611 his crew rebelled and set Henry, his son and seven sailors adrift in icy Hudson Bay— never to be seen again.

Explorers can make a super discovery . . . and not even know it.

In 1492 Christopher Columbus sailed across the Atlantic and landed in Asia—or so he thought. Hey, Christopher, that wasn't Asia. You just landed in the West Indies. Three more voyages to the New World didn't change his mind. He always believed he'd found a new route to Asia.

Son and grandson of Hawaiian missionaries, Hiram Bingham set out to find the ancient Inca city of Vilcabamba. Sure enough, in 1911 he explored stone ruins in the Andes Mountains of Peru. Vilcabamba! It wasn't. Even better, it was the lost Inca City of the Clouds, Machu Picchu.

Explorers can become President, and, yes, Presidents can become explorers, too.

In 1753 George Washington rode three hundred miles into the Ohio Valley Wilderness—in winter. On his return, he had to hike seventy-five miles through deep snow. (His horse couldn't make it.) A fall in the icy Allegheny River and young George almost didn't make it, either.

For seven weeks in 1914, ex-President Teddy Roosevelt paddled through killer rapids down an unexplored river in Brazil's rain forest. A tropical disease nearly killed him. But his adventure paid off. The river now has a name—the Roosevelt River.

As an explorer, think before you speak—your words just might be remembered.

"Dr. Livingstone, I presume?" Henry Stanley blurted out in 1871 when he found explorer David Livingstone in deepest Africa. (Five years before, Dr. L. had discovered Victoria Falls, then disappeared.) Stanley's fancy-dancy greeting is still being laughed at in jokes, skits and comedy routines.

Why would anyone want to climb to the top of the world's highest hill—Mount Everest? British mountaineer George Mallory's reply was down-to-earth: "Because it's there." (On his third attempt in 1924, he lost his life eight hundred feet below the summit.)

Explorers can fail in a quest . . . and still shine as a hero.

Sir Ernest Shackleton, a failure? Well, in three tries he never made it to the South Pole. But in 1916 he sailed eight hundred miles in a lifeboat to save all twenty-seven members of his exploration team, stranded for months on the Arctic ice. That's the stuff of heroes.

First Lady of the Air Amelia Earhart won honors—flying solo across the Atlantic, Hawaii to California, and nonstop across the U.S. In 1937 she had almost completed the first-woman-around-the-world flight when her plane vanished in the Pacific. An American heroine? That's for sure.

You can be an explorer without going anywhere.

Portuguese Prince Henry the Navigator never set sail himself. But in the 1400s, he sent out fifteen expeditions from his headquarters to explore two thousand miles of Africa's west coast. (Vasco da Gama did Henry's explorers one better. He sailed around the tip of Africa to land in India.)

Thanks to Meriwether Lewis and William Clark, President Thomas Jefferson opened the American West—from the White House. In 1803 he sent Lewis and Clark across the United States to find a route to the Pacific Ocean. With the help of their Indian guide Sacagawea, they did.

No question about it—first to reach the highest, deepest, farthest, innermost—is the greatest!

In 1953 Edmund Hillary and Tenzing Norgay climbed 29,035 feet to the summit of the earth's tip-top peak, Mount Everest.

Jacques Piccard and Don Walsh bathysphered down 35,810 feet to the Pacific Ocean's Mariana Trench in 1960 to make the deepest dive ever.

No one has explored farther from Earth—238,754 miles—than Neil Armstrong, Buzz Aldrin and Michael Collins, who barreled off to the moon in 1969.

No one has explored deeper into life's secrets than Francis Collins and Craig Venter, who decoded the human DNA "letters" in 2000.

The age of sailing ships and covered wagons may be over, but some things never change. Explorers still have to be spunky, determined AND follow their vision—like Captain James Cook. On three Pacific voyages in the 1760s and 1770s, British Naval Captain Cook explored and charted more of the earth's surface than anyone up to that time.

That's all well and good for Captain Cook, you say, but there's nothing left to explore. Nonsense! The earth's caves haven't all been explored. Neither have the oceans, the tropical forests, the mountains, the deserts or the inner core of the earth. Outer space is limitless and inner space gene exploration is just beginning.

Grab hold of your vision and get started!

GLOSSARY OF FAMOUS EXPLORERS

Aldrin, Buzz (1930–) New Jersey-born Aldrin joined the Air Force in 1952, flew sixty-six missions in Korea, became an astronaut in 1963 and retired in 1972.

Alexander the Great (356 B.C.–323 B.C.) Crowned king of Macedonia at twenty, Alexander founded an empire that stretched from Greece to northwestern India.

Amundsen, Roald (1872–1928) Norwegian Amundsen also located the exact position of the Magnetic North Pole and explored the Arctic region by air.

Armstrong, Neil (1930–) An aeronautical engineer who served in the Korean War, Ohioan Armstrong flew jets, rockets, helicopters and gliders.

Balboa, Vasco Núñez de (c. 1475–1519) During his nineteen years in the New World, Spanish-born Balboa served as Panama's governor and married a Panamanian.

Barth, Heinrich (1821–1865) After spending many years in North and Central Africa, German explorer Barth wrote a five-volume series about his travels and discoveries.

Bell, Gertrude (1868–1926) Counselor to prime ministers and kings, Arabic-speaking archaeologist Bell helped set the borders of Iraq and choose its king.

Bingham, Hiram (1875–1956) Yale College archaeologist and U.S. senator Bingham led South American expeditions and wrote three books about the Incas of Peru.

Clark, William (1770–1838) After his trip West, Virginia native Clark first became Indian agent for the Louisiana Territory and then governor of Missouri.

Collins, Francis (1950–) Virginian geneticist Collins, who led research that discovered several disease-causing genes, headed up the Human Genome Project.

Collins, Michael (1930–) Born in Rome, Italy, West Point graduate Collins became director of the National Air and Space Museum after retiring from NASA.

Columbus, Christopher (1451–1506) Italian-born Columbus, who found
Spanish financing for his four Western voyages, died in poverty and disgrace.

Cook, James (1728–1779) A farm laborer's son, British naval officer Cook discovered Hawaii and other Pacific islands as well as crossing both the Arctic and Antarctic
circles.

Earhart, Amelia (1897–1937) Kansas-born Earhart, who worked as a nurse's aide during
World War I, devoted her life to flying and setting records.

Eckener, Hugo (1868–1954) German-born Eckener was an aeronautical engineer who also
piloted the first transatlantic airship flight in 1924.

Eriksson, Leif (c. 980–c. 1020) Known as Leif the Lucky, Icelander Eriksson was the son
of the Viking Erik the Red, who explored, settled and named Greenland.

Gagarin, Yuri (1934–1968) Before his death in a plane accident, Russian cosmonaut
Gagarin was named a Hero of the Soviet Union.

da Gama, Vasco (c. 1460–1524) Although soldier and diplomat da Gama was appointed
viceroy of India in 1524 by the Portuguese king, he died shortly after he took office.

de Saussure, Horace (1740–1799) A Swiss mountaineer, geologist, botanist and writer, de
Saussure was also a professor of natural history.

de Soto, Hernando (c. 1496–1542) For two years Spanish conquistador de Soto explored
southeastern America, where he treated the natives with great cruelty.

Henry the Navigator, Prince (1394–1460) Prince Henry's Portuguese seamen added the
Cape Verde Islands and the Azores in the Atlantic Ocean to the world's maps.

Henson, Matthew (1866–1955) Maryland-born African-American Henson knew the Inuit
language, was a skilled dogsled driver and hunted Arctic animals for food.

Herjolfsson, Bjarni (c. 950–?) Icelander Herjolfsson sailed the North Atlantic as a suc-
cessful trader in his ship, called a knarr.

Heyerdahl, Thor (1914–2002) Norwegian Heyerdahl also sailed a raft from Africa to the
West Indies, as well as leading archaeological trips to South America.

Hillary, Edmund (1919–) A New Zealand explorer and mountaineer, Hillary spent many
years in Nepal organizing projects for the benefit of the Sherpas.

Hudson, Henry (c. 1565–1611) The Dutch East India Company paid for English navigator Hudson's four-year effort to find the Northwest Passage.

Jefferson, Thomas (1743–1826) Virginia native Jefferson's 1803 purchase of the Louisiana Territory for $15 million nearly doubled the size of the United States.

Jones, Brian (1947–) With copilot Bertrand Piccard, British-born Jones formed a foundation, Winds of Hope, to benefit ill and suffering Third World children.

Kingsley, Mary (1862–1900) A British traveler and author of two books, Kingsley died of typhoid fever in South Africa while nursing Boer War prisoners.

Kunst, David (1939–) Though Minnesota brothers David and John Kunst started their world trek together, Afghanistan bandits killed John and wounded David.

La Salle, René-Robert Cavelier, Sieur de (1643–c. 1687) While trying to establish a colony in Mississippi, French explorer La Salle was killed by his own followers.

Lewis, Meriwether (1774–1809) Virginian Lewis, who was President Jefferson's White House secretary, was later appointed governor of the Louisiana Territory.

Livingstone, David (1813–1873) A British doctor and missionary, Livingstone spent thirty years exploring Africa, as well as combating disease and slavery.

Magellan, Ferdinand (c. 1480–1521) Born into a noble Portuguese family, Magellan was killed by Philippine natives on his around-the-world voyage.

Mallory, George (1886–1924) A World War I veteran and teacher, Mallory was the only climber to take part in all three British pioneering expeditions to Mount Everest.

Norgay, Tenzing (1914–1986) For twenty years Nepalese Sherpa Norgay served in every expedition that attempted to conquer Mount Everest.

Peary, Robert (1856–1920) In a dispute with Frederick Cook as to who reached the North Pole first, the Navigation Foundation credited Pennsylvanian Peary.

Piccard, Bertrand (1958–) Swiss psychiatrist Piccard is Jacques Piccard's son and the grandson of Auguste Piccard, the first balloonist to reach the stratosphere.

Piccard, Jacques (1922–) Piccard, a Swiss oceanic engineer, also designed the mesoscaphe, which could carry forty people for underwater observation.

Pizarro, Francisco (c. 1476–1541) Born in Spain, Pizarro served twenty years in Caribbean army expeditions before he conquered Peru and founded Lima.

Polo, Marco (1254?–1324?) Italian Polo, who was captured and imprisoned after a 1298 sea battle, dictated his world-famous travel book to a fellow prisoner.

Post, Wiley (1898–1935) Texan Post gave flying exhibitions, flew passenger flights and was a test pilot before losing his life in an Alaskan plane crash.

Powell, John Wesley (1834–1902) A geologist, professor and conservationist, New Yorker Powell lost his right arm fighting for the Union Army in the Civil War.

Pytheas (4th century B.C.) One of the first seamen to fix latitudes, Greek geographer and navigator Pytheas also noted that the tides and the moon were connected.

Roosevelt, Theodore (1858–1919) Although born to wealth in New York City, Roosevelt enjoyed the rugged life, from Western ranching to African safaris.

Sacagawea (c. 1788–1812) With her infant son, Shoshone teenager Sacagawea traveled with Lewis and Clark as guide, interpreter and peace envoy to the Indians.

Scott, Robert (1868–1912) On his fatal attempt to reach the South Pole, British naval captain and explorer Scott kept a diary, which was later published to great acclaim.

Shackleton, Ernest (1874–1922) Irish-born Sir Shackleton, who accompanied Robert Scott on two polar expeditions, was a skilled leader who always put his men first.

Simon, Ted (1931–) A British journalist and author of three books, Simon began a second around-the-world motorcycle trip in 2000 at the age of sixty-nine.

Slocum, Joshua (1844–1909) Born in Nova Scotia, Captain Slocum, who once served as a ship's cook, was lost at sea while attempting a second solo voyage.

Stanley, Henry (1841–1904) Welshman Stanley, sent by an American newspaper to find David Livingstone, spent the next ten years in further African exploration.

Stevens, Thomas (1854–1935) A native of Great Britain, Stevens worked in the United States as a miner and rancher before his cycling adventure.

Venter, J. Craig (1946–) Although Vietnam veteran Venter was in competition with Collins, the two men jointly announced success of the Human Genome Project.

Vespucci, Amerigo (1454–1512) Born into a wealthy Italian family, merchant-explorer Vespucci was the first to declare that South America was a new continent.

Walsh, Don (1931–) A marine engineer and graduate of the U.S. Naval Academy, Californian Walsh followed a lifelong career in oceanic studies.

Washburn, Barbara (1914–) Washburn and her husband, Bradford, also mapped mountain ranges as well as spending seven years mapping the Grand Canyon.

Washington, George (1732–1799) Virginia-born Washington spent much of his youth in the wilderness, both as a surveyor and on military expeditions.

White, James (1882–1946) Texas native White was not only the first to explore Carlsbad Caverns, but he was also the Caverns' chief guide for many years.

Yeager, Charles (1923–) West Virginian Yeager also flew combat missions in Vietnam, retiring as a Brigadier General in 1975 after a distinguished flying career.

BIBLIOGRAPHY

Bryan, C.D.B. *The National Geographic Society: 100 Years of Adventure and Discovery.* New York: Harry N. Abrams, Inc., 1987.

Edmonds, Jane, Ed. *Oxford Atlas of Exploration.* London: Reed International Books Limited, George Philip Limited, 1997.

Fleming, Fergus. *Killing Dragons: The Conquest of the Alps.* New York: Atlantic Monthly Press, 2000.

Fritz, Jean. *Around the World in a Hundred Years: From Henry the Navigator to Magellan.* New York: G. P. Putnam's Sons, 1994.

Kagan, Hilde Heun, Ed. *The American Heritage Pictorial Atlas of United States History.* New York: American Heritage Publishing Co., Inc., 1966.

Leithauser, Joachim G. *Worlds Beyond the Horizon.* New York: Alfred A. Knopf, 1955.

Morison, Samuel Eliot. *The European Discovery of America: The Northern Voyages A.D. 500–1600.* New York: Oxford University Press, 1971.

Roberts, Gail. *Atlas of Discovery.* New York: Crown Publishers, Inc., 1973.

Whittingham, Richard. *The Rand McNally Almanac of Adventure.* Chicago: Rand McNally & Company, 1982.

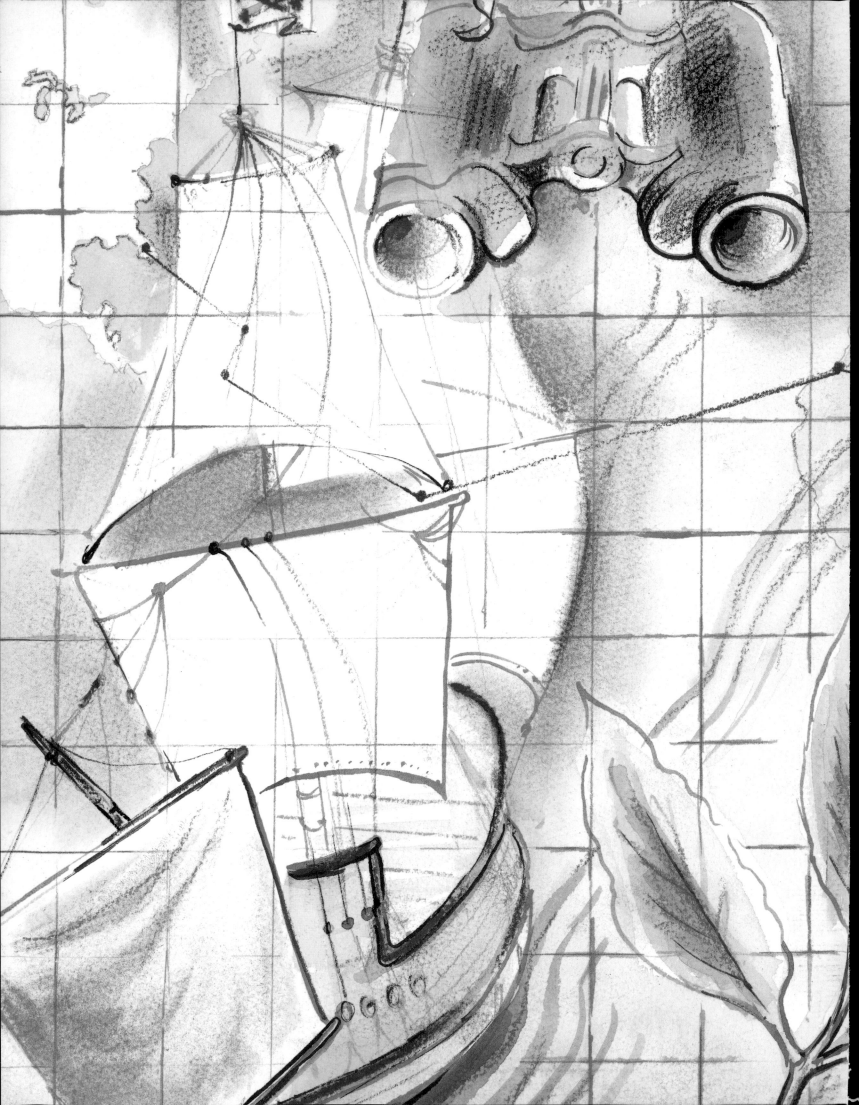